LONDON'S COLOURFUL PAGEANTRY

A Month-by-Month Guide

Text by Rachel Stewart

The **Changing of the Guard** is the most popular of London's ceremonies. Indeed, what could be more stirring than the spectacle of the Old Guard lined up on Buckingham Palace forecourt, dressed in their scarlet tunics and black bearskins, while the steady beat of the corps of drums heralds the arrival of the St James's Palace contingent! They march in through the south centre gate, their colour solemnly borne by an ensign. At almost 11.30 am the rousing music of the regimental band of the New Guard can be heard and the men enter by the north centre gate. Sharp commands from the drill sergeant ring out across the forecourt. The New Guard advances in slow time towards the Old, then the symbolic ceremony of handing over the palace keys takes place between the two captains. After orders have been given and sentries posted, the Old Guard leaves for their barracks in quick time. Shortly afterwards, the senior detachment of the New Guard marches away to St James's Palace, leaving the Buckingham Palace detachment to begin its duties.

BELOW: The New Guard prepares for duty at Windsor Castle.

ABOVE: A mounted trooper of the Life Guards in ceremonial uniform.

The men of The Queen's Guard are not just trained for ceremonial duty. They are tough fighting soldiers ready for active service in any part of the world. There are five foot regiments, which can be distinguished by the plumes in their bearskin caps and the arrangement of buttons on their tunics. The Grenadier Guards have a white plume and evenly spaced buttons, the Coldstream Guards have a red plume and buttons in pairs, while the buttons of the Scots Guards are in threes, but they have no plume; the Irish Guards wear a blue plume in their bearskins, and have tunic buttons in fours, whereas the plume of the Welsh Guards is green and white and buttons are in fives.

Guard mounting can also be seen at the Tower of London at 11.30 am on the same days as the other two

ABOVE: Yeomen Warders of the Tower.

ABOVE: Led by its regimental band and corps of drums, the Old Guard leaves Buckingham Palace and returns to barracks, its period of duty completed.

palaces, that is daily in summer (unless very wet) and on alternate days in the autumn and winter. Further guard mounting of foot soldiers can be viewed at Windsor Castle. In winter, the red tunics are replaced with long grey coats.

The Household Division is completed by two mounted regiments, the Life Guards and the Blues and Royals. They take it in turns to provide the guard in Whitehall and the mounting ceremony can be viewed at Horse Guards at 11 am (Sundays 10 am). The scarlet tunics and the gleaming swords, cuirasses, and helmets with waving plumes all add to this colourful spectacle.

BELOW: As the Chief Warder raises his Tudor bonnet, the Ceremony of the Keys draws to a close.

Taking place in the late evening, beneath the gloomy walls of the Tower of London, the **Ceremony of the Keys** has a special atmosphere. After locking the gates of the Middle and Byward Towers, the Chief Yeoman Warder, distinctive in his red coat and Tudor bonnet, proceeds with his guard to the archway of the Bloody Tower. 'Halt, who comes there?' challenges the sentry, and the Chief Warder replies 'The Keys'. 'Whose Keys?' 'Queen Elizabeth's Keys.' The sentry finally says, 'Pass, Queen Elizabeth's Keys, all's well,' and the guard presents arms. The bugle sounds the lone call of the Last Post and the Keys are conveyed to the Resident Governor at the Queen's House.

ABOVE: *One of the highlights of Chinese New Year is the fabulous 'Lion' Dance.*

ABOVE: *Celebrating the protected Chinese panda.*

The **New Year** opens with an animated parade around the West End, in which vigorous marching bands set the tempo, and the Lord Mayors of Westminster take the opportunity of greeting their citizens.

By contrast, a quiet and dignified ceremony, more than 900 years old, takes place on Twelfth Day in the Chapel Royal of St James's Palace. This is the **Royal Epiphany Gifts Service** in which the three wise men of the East are remembered. Two Gentlemen Ushers, who represent The Queen, are led to the altar by the Serjeant of the Vestry. They bring with them the traditional Epiphany gifts of gold, frankincense and myrrh. Behind them is an escort of Serjeant Major and two Yeomen of the Guard. After the service the gold is exchanged for currency and given to charity.

Charles I's execution is commemorated by the King's Army of the English Civil War Society on the last Sunday in January. Dressed in authentic Royalist style, they gather at St James's Palace and march along the route taken by the king before his

BELOW: *A forty-metre dragon weaves its way through the streets.*

ABOVE: *Boat Race crew.*

death at the scaffold at the Banqueting House, Whitehall. Here a wreath is laid.

If you suffer from a throat ailment, you can be blessed at the Church of St Etheldreda in Ely Place, and the priest will lay two unlit candles against the affected part. This occurs on the feast of St Blaise, who reputedly saved the life of a child with a fishbone stuck in his throat.

On the afternoon of the first Sunday in February, there is an astonishing sight in an east London church (generally Holy Trinity, E8). Dozens of clowns assemble, dressed in their bright costumes, with white faces and large red smiles. They remember their originator, Grimaldi, and afterwards perform for the public in the church hall.

Another colourful event is the **Chinese New Year**. Gay banners and streamers decorate the streets of Soho and onlookers are treated to displays of kung fu and the popular 'Lion' dances, in which several men dress up as a large monster.

Rowing enthusiasts are well catered for in the early spring. Mortlake to Putney is the course for 420 boats competing in the Head of the River Race, while the two crews of the Oxford and Cambridge Boat Race row in the reverse direction. Thousands of people jostle for vantage points along the riverside to cheer for their favourite university, while others pay for fine views from barges.

RIGHT: *Straining at the oars to be Head of the River.*

ABOVE: *At the Widow's Son Inn.*

ABOVE: *A touch of humour at the London Marathon.*

A rather pathetic memorial takes place at the Widow's Son Inn at Bow. In the eighteenth century, a cottage used to stand here, belonging to a widow. Expecting her sailor son to return home from sea on Good Friday she put out a hot cross bun for him. But he never came back. So she hung the bun from her beam. Undeterred, she continued to put out a bun each year, and the uneaten ones she added to her growing collection hanging from the ceiling. Her loving tribute is continued to this day.

If Easter falls early, then the scantily clad beauty queens at the **Battersea Park Parade** usually suffer from goosepimples. This is a very jolly affair, with glorious flower floats, brass bands and a wide variety of entertainments. Although officially begun as recently as 1962, it continues a custom of Victorian ladies, who promenaded in the park to show off their new Easter bonnets.

In Regent's Park on Easter Monday, working horses demonstrate their skills at pulling brewers' drays, large commercial vans, private carriages and small traps. The culmination is the grand **Harness Horse Parade**, consisting of the best in each class.

Thousands of fitness enthusiasts assemble at Greenwich to compete in the **London Marathon**, a gruelling twenty-seven mile course along the streets to Westminster Bridge. Most have been training for months, if not years beforehand, the aim being to stagger somehow to the finishing line. Friends and relatives line the route to encourage the faint-hearted and provide sustaining orange juice.

Historians will be fascinated by the memorial service at St Andrew Undershaft for John Stow, who wrote *The Survey of London* in 1598. He was so carried away by his historical

ABOVE: *John Stow, famous historian.*

RIGHT: *Easter Parade, Battersea Park.*

studies that he neglected his trade of master tailor and became poverty-stricken. James I granted him a beggar's licence, so that his important researches could continue. An eminent historian gives an address and a new quill pen is placed in the hand of Stow's statue by the Lord Mayor.

On the Thursday after Easter, the Lord Mayor with the Sheriffs and Aldermen of the City of London can be seen in full regalia when they process from the Guildhall to the nearby church of St Lawrence Jewry. Here they listen to the **Spital Sermon** (named after the Hospital of St Mary Spital), which has an Easter theme.

A more solemn procession is the **Tyburn Walk** from the Old Bailey, which commemorates the martyrdom of Catholics at the gallows in the sixteenth and seventeenth centuries.

BELOW: *Beating the Bounds of the parish, at the Tower of London.*

ABOVE: A drummer of the Household Cavalry at Windsor.

ABOVE: Prince Philip competing in the Royal Windsor Horse Show.

Windsor Castle provides an imposing backdrop to the **Royal Windsor Horse Show**, founded in 1943. Marquees cluster around the show-jumping ring, offering refreshments and selling everything from souvenirs to saddles. Members of the Royal Family have competed enthusiastically here including Prince Philip, who has frequently proved his skills in the International Driving Grand Prix. Spectators are also treated to special displays of royal horses and carriages, and a popular event is the heart-warming Musical Ride of the Household Cavalry.

Punch and Judy shows have provided entertainment for all ages for more than a century and two festivals in Covent Garden attract puppeteers from all over the country, one in May and the other in September or October. The glove puppets are traditionally operated by the 'Professor', dressed in loud checked or striped trousers, with colourful top hat and tails, assisted by the 'Bottler', who involves the audience in the action and takes the hat round afterwards. The plots vary, but generally include the characters of Punch, his wife Judy, their baby, the butcher and the policeman.

For four days in May, gardening enthusiasts congregate in the grounds of the Royal Hospital, Chelsea, to enjoy the glorious colours and perfumes of the thousands of blooms at the famous **Flower Show**. Every

RIGHT: Theme gardens, Chelsea Flower Show.

ABOVE: *The Chelsea Flower Show.*

kind of plant can be seen, from the exotic shapes of miniature Bonsai trees to stately rows of giant delphiniums. Complete gardens are also laid out, each with a theme, to give the public some inspiration for plantings at home. The Royal Horticultural Society, which runs the show, provides a bureau where advice can be sought concerning any type of gardening problem. On the last day, plants and cut flowers can be purchased. The Chelsea Flower Show has been a favourite event with Londoners, since its inception in 1913.

Two kings are honoured this month. On 21 May, representatives of Eton College and King's College, Cambridge, meet at the Wakefield Tower, Tower of London, to remember their founder, Henry VI. They place white **lilies and roses** on the spot where he was supposedly murdered in 1471.

On the Thursday after 29 May, known as **Oak Apple Day**, the Chelsea Pensioners honour Charles II, founder of the Royal Hospital where they live. All former soldiers, they decorate his statue with oak leaves and branches. This commemorates his escape after the battle of Worcester in 1651, when he hid in an oak tree. The Pensioners parade in their eighteenth-century-style scarlet coats, proudly displaying their medals, and wearing their distinctive black tricorne hats with gold trimming.

RIGHT: *Founder's Day, Royal Hospital, Chelsea.*

Impressive military displays highlight this month, starting with **Beating Retreat**, performed by the Household Division on Horse Guards Parade. The term refers to the retreat of sunlight. The five regiments of Foot Guards provide a superb demonstration of their marching and drilling expertise to the spirited music of the brass bands, with trumpets, pipes and drums, while the two mounted regiments of Life Guards and Blues and Royals add a natural elegance. The floodlit evening performances have a particularly magical atmosphere.

A few days later, there is a second Beating or Sounding Retreat by a different Division, the massed bands providing the biggest attraction.

Trooping the Colour, which marks The Queen's official birthday, is probably the greatest parade of all. The ceremony evolved from the display of the regimental flag to the soldiers, so that they would instantly recognize it on the battlefield. The sovereign's birthday has been honoured in this way since 1805.

The Queen leaves Buckingham Palace mid-morning and rides down The Mall to Horse Guards Parade, accompanied by the Sovereign's Escort of the Household Cavalry. The National Anthem is played by the massed mounted bands, resplendent in their golden tunics, and a gun salute is fired in Green Park. The guards drill in both slow and quick time, but the central part of the ceremony begins

Far left: *The immaculate drill of the guards at Trooping the Colour, Horse Guards Parade.*

Left: *After Trooping the Colour, the Royal Family gathers on the balcony of Buckingham Palace for the fly-past.*

Below: *Officer of the Blues and Royals at Trooping the Colour.*

when a lone drummer leaves the other musicians to beat the 'Drummer's Call' to the Escort for the Colour. The colour is trooped down the entire line of guards to the rousing tune of 'The Grenadiers' March', then all regiments pay their respects to Her Majesty before the return procession up The Mall.

At one o'clock The Queen appears on the balcony of Buckingham Palace with members of her family, to view the fly-past given by the RAF.

The **Order of the Garter**, an ancient order of chivalry, was founded in 1348 by Edward III to celebrate his victories over the kings of Scotland and France, who were both imprisoned at Windsor. No one knows exactly why such an intimate article became the emblem for this noble order, but, according to one traditional story, the blue garter belonged to a famous beauty, Joan, Countess of Salisbury, possibly the king's mistress, who later married his son, the Black Prince. During a ball in 1347, which was held to celebrate the capture of Calais, the lady's garter fell to the ground. When the king picked it up, some of the courtiers smiled knowingly, which prompted Edward to say, *'Honi soit qui mal y pense'* ('Shame on him who thinks evil of it'). He then declared that it would be advanced to 'high honour and estimation'.

Thus, twenty-four of the most outstanding military leaders of the day were installed as Knights of the Garter, which brought them together in close companionship with the sovereign. A three-day festival was

LEFT: On the steps of St George's Chapel after the Garter Installation Service.

BELOW: The Queen and Prince Philip acknowledge the crowds.

ABOVE: *The Garter Day procession.*

held, which included meeting in Chapter, banquets, and services in St George's Chapel.

The six-hundredth anniversary of the Order was celebrated in 1948, when King George VI commanded the knights to assemble at Windsor, process through the castle precincts and hold a service together. Since then, a Garter Day has been held annually and the Knights Companion wear their robes of Garter blue and hats with curling white plumes.

New knights are appointed by the sovereign from among people who have made a special contribution to the life of the nation, and they are invested with their robes and insignia in the Garter Throne Room. This room was converted into a place of assembly for the knights during the reign of King George IV, and the theme colour of blue is retained in the carpet and upholstery of the elegant chairs and stools. After the investiture, the knights process through the castle to St George's Chapel for their installation service. The Honourable Corps of Gentlemen at Arms and the Yeomen of the Guard are generally in attendance, wearing their splendid uniforms, and bands of the Household Division provide the stirring music.

DAILY CEREMONIES

Changing the Guard, Buckingham Palace, St James's Palace, the Tower of London and Windsor Castle (*alternate days August to end March*)
Mounting the Guard, Horse Guards, Whitehall, SW1
Ceremony of the Keys, Tower of London EC3

JANUARY

Lord Mayors of Westminster's New Year's Day Parade *(1st)*
Royal Epiphany Gifts Service, Chapel Royal, St James's Palace *(6th)*
Court of Common Council: procession and service, Church of St Lawrence Jewry, EC2
Charles I Commemoration, Banqueting House, Whitehall *(last Sunday)*

FEBRUARY

Chinese New Year *(or late January)*
Blessing of the Throats Service, Church of St Etheldreda, EC1 *(3rd)*
Clowns' Service, Holy Trinity Church, E8 *(1st Sunday)*
Gun Salute – Accession Day *(6th)*
Scouts and Guides Founders' Day Service, Westminster Abbey *(Saturday nearest 22nd)*
Crufts Dog Show, Earls Court, SW5

MARCH

Head of the River Race, Mortlake to Putney *(3rd or 4th Saturday)*
Oxford v Cambridge University Boat Race, Putney to Mortlake *(Saturday, or April)*
Cakes and Ale Sermon, St Paul's Cathedral: procession and service *(Ash Wednesday)*
Commonwealth Day Observance Service, Westminster Abbey *(12th)*
Oranges and Lemons Children's Service, Church of St Clement Danes, WC2 *(28th)*

APRIL

Hot Cross Buns Service, St Bartholomew-the-Great Church, EC1 *(Good Friday)*
Hot Cross Bun Ceremony, Widow's Son Inn, 75 Devons Road, E3 *(Good Friday)*
Easter Parade, Battersea Park, SW11 *(Easter Sunday)*
Harness Horse Parade, Regents Park, NW1 *(Easter Monday)*
London Marathon, Greenwich to Westminster Bridge
John Stow's Quill Pen Ceremony, Church of St Andrew Undershaft, EC3 *(on or near 5th)*
Spital Sermon Procession, Guildhall to Church of St Lawrence Jewry, EC2 *(1st Thursday after Easter)*
Gun Salute – The Queen's Birthday *(21st)*
Tyburn Walk, Old Bailey to Tyburn Convent *(last Sunday)*

MAY

Beating the Bounds, Tower of London *(every 3 years)* and All Hallows by the Tower, EC3 *(every year) (Ascension Day)*
Historic Commercial Vehicle Run, Crystal Palace Park *(7th)*
Punch and Judy Festival, Covent Garden, WC2 *(2nd Sunday)*
Royal Windsor Horse Show, Home Park, Windsor *(mid-May)*
British Heart Foundation's Run, Walk, Jog, Tower of London, EC3 *(17th)*
Ceremony of the Lilies and Roses, Tower of London *(21st)*
Dick Whittington Charity Walk, from Pauntley, Glos *(21st)* finishing at Guildhall, EC2 on June 5th
Chelsea Flower Show, Royal Hospital, Chelsea, SW3 *(late May)*
Oak Apple Day, Royal Hospital, Chelsea, SW3 *(Thursday after 29th)*
Cycling: Milk Race, Westminster Bridge *(29th)*

JUNE

Gun Salute – Coronation Day *(2nd)*
Beating Retreat, Horse Guards Parade
Derby Day, Epsom, Surrey *(Wednesday of 1st week)*
Gun Salute – Duke of Edinburgh's Birthday *(10th)*
The Queen's Birthday Parade – Trooping the Colour, Horse Guards Parade *(2nd Saturday)*
Biggin Hill International Air Fair, Biggin Hill, Kent
The Garter Ceremony, Windsor Castle *(mid-June)*
Royal Ascot, Ascot, Berkshire *(3rd week, Tuesday to Friday)*
Wimbledon Lawn Tennis Championships, All England Lawn Tennis Club, SW19 *(late June)*
The Knollys Red Rose Rent, All Hallows by the Tower, EC3
Henley Royal Regatta, Henley-on-Thames, Oxon. *(week before 27th Sunday)*
Royal Garden Parties, Buckingham Palace

JULY

City of London Festival
Order of St Michael and St George Service, St Paul's Cathedral *(2nd week)*
Royal Tournament, Earls Court, SW5 *(mid-July)*
Installation of the Grand Master of the Vintners: Road-Sweeping Ceremony *(2nd Wednesday)*
BBC Henry Wood Promenade Concerts, Royal Albert Hall, SW7 *(July to September)*
Swan Upping *(3rd week)*
Doggett's Coat and Badge Race, London Bridge to Chelsea *(late July)*

AUGUST

Gun Salute – the Queen Mother's Birthday *(4th)*
Notting Hill Carnival, Ladbroke Grove, W11 *(Bank Holiday Sunday and Monday)*
London Riding Horse Parade, Rotten Row, Hyde Park, W2 *(6th)*
Westminster Horse Show, Hyde Park, W2 *(26th – 28th)*
Charity Fun day, Tower Bridge, SE1 *(28th)*

SEPTEMBER

Blue Coat Boys' March, St Sepulchre's, EC1 to Guildhall *(21st)*
Admission of Sheriffs: procession, Mansion House to Guildhall *(28th or preceding Friday)*
Election of the Lord Mayor, Guildhall, EC2 *(on or near 29th, Michaelmas Day)*
Punch and Judy Festival, Covent Garden Piazza, WC2 *(last Sunday or 1st Sunday October)*

OCTOBER

Quit-Rents Ceremony, Royal Courts of Justice, WC2 *(early October)*
Pearly Kings and Queens, Costermongers' Harvest Festival, St Martin-in-the Fields, WC2 *(1st Sunday)*
Fish Harvest Festival, Church of St Mary-at-Hill, EC3 *(2nd Sunday)*
Lion Sermon, St Katharine Cree Church, EC3 *(on or near 16th)*
Opening of the Law Courts: procession
Horse of the Year Show, Wembley Arena, Wembley
State Opening of Parliament (including Searching the Cellars), Palace of Westminster *(late October or early November)*

NOVEMBER

London to Brighton Veteran Car Run, Hyde Park, W2 *(1st Sunday)*
Remembrance Sunday, Cenotaph, Whitehall, SW1 *(2nd Sunday)*
Installation of the Lord Mayor: procession, Mansion House to Guildhall *(2nd Friday)*
Silent Ceremony, Guildhall, EC2 *(2nd Friday)*
Lord Mayor's Show, City of London *(2nd Saturday)*
Festival of St Cecilia Service, St Sepulchre's, EC1 *(on or near 22nd)*

DECEMBER

Royal Smithfield Show, Earls Court, SW5
Christmas Tree, Trafalgar Square, WC2 *(mid-December to early January)*
Olympia International Showjumping Championships, Olympia, W14

ABOVE: *Men's doubles, Wimbledon.*

LEFT: *The Royal Enclosure, Ascot.*

Two famous race meetings, both dating from the eighteenth century, draw the crowds in June. Parties of Londoners head for the Epsom Race Course on **Derby Day**, the Wednesday of the first week. Here they unpack their picnic baskets, or treat themselves to tubs of jellied eel, and have a flutter with the 'Bookies'. Excitement is intense as the jockeys flash by in their vivid colours and the spectators cheer their favourites to the finishing line. Afterwards, everyone enjoys the rides and sideshows of the funfair.

BELOW: *Wimbledon's grass courts.*

ABOVE: *Finishing line, Henley Regatta.*

LEFT: *A quiet picnic, Henley.*

Royal Ascot, started by Queen Anne in 1711, represents the height of 'The Season', especially on the Thursday, known as 'Ladies Day' or 'Gold Cup Day', when the many fabulous hats worn by spectators seem to receive more attention than the horses. The Queen and other members of the Royal Family drive from Windsor in open landaus, then on down the course before racing begins. Formal attire is compulsory in the Royal Enclosure, and the gentlemen look exceedingly elegant in their top hats.

Also world famous are the **Wimbledon** Lawn Tennis Championships, when international tennis stars compete for a full fortnight for the coveted titles. Opened by King George V in 1922, the complex includes thirty grass courts made of cherished Cumberland turf. The Centre Court is the arena for the most exciting finals, and a ticket here is highly prized. Helping to ease the tension are the strawberries and champagne, the traditional refreshments.

Another fashionable event, begun in 1839, is the **Henley** Royal Regatta, when the Thames once again provides the course. Competitors row against the current for one mile almost up to Henley Bridge. Blazers and straw boaters are the customary wear for smart young men, while the ladies flaunt their prettiest summer dresses.

The three **Royal Garden Parties** have taken the place of débutantes' balls, and members of the Royal Family have the opportunity of meeting deserving people on these delightful occasions. Tea is provided for some 9,000 guests, who drift around the vast lawns of Buckingham Palace gardens and admire the flamingoes on the lake.

The most spectacular event this month is the **Royal Tournament**, held at the Earls Court Centre for two and a half weeks. Since 1880, the armed forces have provided the action, thrilling displays and competitions – all in aid of charity. Members of the Royal Family, as patrons, attend and take the salute.

The Queen can also be seen by the public when she goes to the annual service of the **Order of St Michael and St George** at St Paul's Cathedral. As Sovereign of the Order, she wears a long blue cloak lined with red and the train is carried by a page boy. Founded in 1818, the Order is awarded for distinguished endeavour overseas.

Music lovers have a feast of concerts from July until September at the **'Proms'**, which take place at the Royal Albert Hall. Promenaders can enjoy a variety of music at reasonable prices. Sir Henry Wood was involved in the conducting and planning of programmes from the first year in 1895 until 1944, after which the BBC took over the organization. Tickets for the last night, which has a patriotic atmosphere, are allocated to regular attenders. Flags are waved and old favourites such as 'Land of Hope and Glory' are sung with fervour.

ABOVE: *Swan uppers at Boulter's Lock.*

BELOW: *Road Sweeping procession.*

The Vintners' Company, an ancient livery company of the City of London, is in evidence on two occasions in July. The first is their quaint **Road Sweeping Ceremony**, when the newly elected Master, Wardens and Court of Assistants walk in procession from their hall in Upper Thames Street, to their church, St James's in Garlickhythe. According to a centuries-old tradition, the Wine Tackle Porter sweeps the road ahead of them with a broom, to remove the 'foulness and litter'. Additionally, all are provided with nosegays of sweet herbs so that 'their nostrils be not offended'. The Wine Porter wears a top hat and smock. The Bargemaster is also present in his ceremonial black and silver frock coat.

For the **Swan Upping** ceremony, the Bargemaster's outfit is more practical, consisting of a green blazer, white trousers and naval cap. Five

ABOVE: Outrageous fancy dress characterises the Notting Hill Carnival.

RIGHT: Former winners of the Doggett's Coat and Badge sculling race.

hundred of the swans on the Thames belong to The Queen and the rest to the Vintners' and Dyers' Companies, and all the cygnets have to be counted, caught and marked with nicks in their beaks. The eighteen watermen are led by the Royal Swan Keeper, a post first established in about 1300.

The oldest boat race in England is the **Doggett's Coat and Badge Race**, rowed the five miles between London Bridge and Chelsea with single sculls. The participants are six members of the Watermen's Company and the winner is presented with the highly prized scarlet uniform, with large silver badge on the left sleeve. Thomas Doggett, an Irish comedian, founded the race in 1715 to express his thanks to a young waterman who rowed him safely home one stormy evening after the theatre.

The **Notting Hill Carnival** is an exuberant West Indian two-day event, originally started for children in 1965. The streets come alive with gaily dressed dancers and singers gyrating to the sound of steel and brass bands.

ABOVE: *Aldermen and officers of livery companies process to St Lawrence Jewry.*

ABOVE: *Town criers take part in ceremonial functions, but no longer proclaim the news.*

Christ's Hospital, Newgate Street, was founded in 1553 by Edward VI as an orphanage. The yellow colour of the stockings, which the boys still wear, was supposed to deter the rats from biting their ankles! The nickname **'Bluecoat Boys'** comes from their distinctive uniform. In 1902, the school moved to Horsham in Sussex, but on St Matthew's Day about 400 pupils return for a service with the Lord Mayor and Aldermen at St Sepulchre's, Holborn. Afterwards they march in procession, accompanied by the school band, to Guildhall. They have lunch there and each receives a small gift.

BELOW: *High Court judges, prior to opening the new legal year.*

Two Sheriffs are elected annually on Midsummer's Day from among the Aldermen of the City. For their formal admission to office in September, they process from the Mansion House to Guildhall, along with the Lord Mayor and fellow liverymen. They are then presented with their chains of office.

On or near Michaelmas Day, the new Lord Mayor is elected. Ever since 1406, the election of Richard Whittington, the serving Mayor and his entourage have processed to St Lawrence Jewry, carrying posies of old-fashioned English flowers. There they ask for guidance, and then continue on to the Guildhall. Inside the splendid medieval Great Hall, the liverymen are assembled. The names of two candidates are read out, selected from among past Sheriffs, and the Aldermen decide on the final one. The City bells ring out as the Lord Mayor and his successor ride in the golden horse-drawn coach to the Mansion House, the Lord Mayor's official residence, built in 1739.

Cockney costermongers, or street traders, have held very different elections since 1880. **Pearly Kings and Queens** have been chosen to safeguard the rights of stall-holders. Their gleaming costumes consist of hundreds of pearl buttons sewn in intricate patterns, on to their hats, jackets, waistcoats, trousers or skirts. They often support charities, and can be seen at several events, including their harvest festival service which takes place at St Martin-in-the-Fields.

Since the seventeenth century, another unusual **harvest festival** has been held in the church of St Mary-at-Hill near the former Billingsgate fish market. Today, merchants from the newly sited market on the Isle of Dogs display a wide variety of fish in the vestibule, and the service is attended by the Aldermen and Councilmen clad in full regalia.

ABOVE: Pearly Harvest Festival.

At the Royal Courts of Justice a quaint thirteenth-century custom is enacted by the Comptroller of the City Corporation. He pays a **quit-rent** for two holdings: for the moors in Shropshire a blunt billhook and a sharp hatchet, and for a former forge in St Clement Danes six horseshoes and sixty-one nails (thought to originate from jousts held nearby).

A somewhat extraordinary sermon has been preached every year for the last three centuries at St Katharine Cree. It concerns a trader, Sir John Gayer, whose prayers prevented an attack by a lion when he was lost in the desert in the Near East.

LEFT: Dyed and curled ostrich feathers adorn the hats of Pearly Queens.

Although the public is not admitted to the **State Opening of Parliament** itself, thousands of spectators line the route from Buckingham Palace, down The Mall and Whitehall, to the Palace of Westminster, in the hope of catching a glimpse of The Queen and the Duke of Edinburgh driving by in the Australian State Coach. Ahead of The Queen's procession is another State Coach, Queen Alexandra's, which conveys the Imperial State Crown, the Sword of State and the Cap of Maintenance used at the ceremony.

Before their arrival at the Palace of Westminster, the Yeomen of the Guard have searched the cellars by the light of lanterns, to make sure that no modern Guy Fawkes has been planning to blow up Parliament.

A royal salute is fired by the King's Troop of the Royal Horse Artillery in Hyde Park and The Queen and other members of her family enter the Houses of Parliament through the great arch under the Victoria Tower. Then The Queen puts on the Imperial State Crown and royal robes with long red train in the Robing Room, which has on its walls five huge frescoes of Arthurian legend. To the sound of trumpets, she is conducted to the House of Lords where she ascends the red-carpeted dais to the throne. The Lords are present in their splendid robes. The Gentleman Usher of the Black Rod knocks three times on the door leading to the Commons and requests admittance. He summons the members of the Commons, who enter, led by the Speaker wearing his full-bottomed wig and his robe of black satin damask trimmed with gold. Then The Queen reads her speech which outlines the government's policies. This part of the ritual can be traced back to the mid-thirteenth century.

TOP: Queen Alexandra's State Coach conveys the Imperial State Crown.

LEFT: The crown is carried to Her Majesty.

RIGHT: The Royal Procession moves to the State Opening of Parliament.

ABOVE: *The Lord Mayor's fairytale coach was constructed in 1757.*

Only the very oldest cars, made during the ten years between 1895 and 1905, are allowed to enter the London to Brighton **Veteran Car Run**. Polished until they gleam, the cars are cranked up for the start at Hyde Park Corner in the early morning, arriving in Madeira Drive, Brighton, hopefully, some three hours later. Drivers dress for the part in goggles and plus-fours, while passengers wrap themselves in rugs. The run celebrates the abolition of the law which decreed that a man carrying a warning red flag should walk ahead of all motor vehicles.

Meanwhile, activity in the City is reaching fever pitch, as final preparations are made for the **Lord Mayor's Show**. The day before, the new Lord Mayor is officially installed in a ceremony called the 'Silent Change'. Years ago, the election used to cause such violent outbursts, that a rule of silence had to be made. Thus, the outgoing Lord Mayor hands over his Mace, Crystal Sceptre, Seal and sixteenth-century Privy Purse without saying a word.

The purpose of the Show, more than 700 years old, is for the new Lord Mayor to greet his people and to take his oath of office at the Royal Courts of Justice. Six powerful white horses pull the elaborate gilded coach, from which the Lord Mayor waves his hat to the

LEFT: *Fireworks cascade above the dome of St Paul's Cathedral.*

RIGHT: *Veteran cars set out for their annual run to Brighton.*

ABOVE: *A dazzling gift to Londoners from the people of Norway.*

ABOVE: *A solemn moment at the Cenotaph on Remembrance Sunday.*

citizens of the City. Members of the Honourable Artillery Company, dressed as pikemen and musketeers of the Civil War in red tunics and shining breastplates and helmets, walk either side of the coach as guardsmen. Dozens of decorated floats, many sponsored by livery companies, take part in the procession, which has a theme, such as a good cause or topic of national importance. Regimental bands add to the joyful atmosphere.

A moving ceremony takes place on **Remembrance Sunday** in Whitehall. War veterans and members of the armed forces assemble around the Cenotaph Memorial and The Queen and other members of the Royal Family, and government and Services representatives lay wreaths there in memory of those who gave their lives in the World Wars. A two-minute silence is observed at 11 am, marked by a gun fired from Horse Guards Parade.

The patron saint of music, **Saint Cecilia**, is honoured at St Sepulchre's in Holborn, where leading organists and choristers gather to perform the most glorious church music in a sixteenth-century ceremony.

In mid-December the people of Oslo present an enormous **Christmas tree** to Londoners, which is erected in Trafalgar Square and decorated with many sparkling white lights. This becomes a focal point for **carol singing** in aid of charities. On New Year's Eve there are riotous celebrations here rounded off by a noisy rendering of 'Auld Lang Syne'. Fairy lights entice shoppers to the West End until Twelfth Night.

ABOVE: *Banquet in the magnificence of St George's Hall, Windsor Castle.*

Heads of State do not make private visits to Britain unless they have already made an official **State Visit**. The Queen acts as hostess inviting him or her to stay at one of her residences. If this is to be Buckingham Palace, then there is great activity at the Royal Mews, preparing the carriages, horses and State livery for the formal procession that acts as a greeting. Similarly, if the visitor is staying at Windsor Castle, there will

LEFT: *An honour is conferred at Buckingham Palace by Prince Charles.*

ABOVE: Band of the Scots Guards heralds a State Visit.

ABOVE: Inspection of the Scots Guards by the King of Spain.

be a magnificent carriage procession through the Home Park and, in fine weather, it is likely that The Queen will drive with her guest in the 1902 State Landau. Later, a glittering banquet will be held in honour of the visiting Head of State, with many dignitaries seated both sides of a vast table, waited upon by footmen.

Gun salutes, which commemorate various royal events, take place in Hyde Park (fired by the King's Troop, Royal Horse Artillery – forty-one rounds) and at the Tower of London (fired by the Honourable Artillery Company – sixty-two rounds). The horses galloping across the park, pulling the six gun carriages behind them, create a fine spectacle.

The Queen and other senior members of the Royal Family regularly conduct the ceremony for the conferment of honours, held in the Ball Room at Buckingham Palace. Each recipient has to walk up to the elegant throne dais surmounted by a crimson canopy to receive the honour, of which there are several, from knighthoods to the Order of the British Empire.

Whenever The Queen visits the City in State, a medieval ceremony is repeated which acknowledges the overlordship of the sovereign. At the site of the old Temple Bar, the Lord Mayor waits with the ancient Pearl Sword and Mace. On The Queen's arrival, he offers her the hilt of the sword to touch. The Aldermen and Lord Mayor then go ahead of the sovereign to lead her into the City.

RIGHT: The King's Troop honours Prince Philip's birthday with a gun salute.

Map of Central London

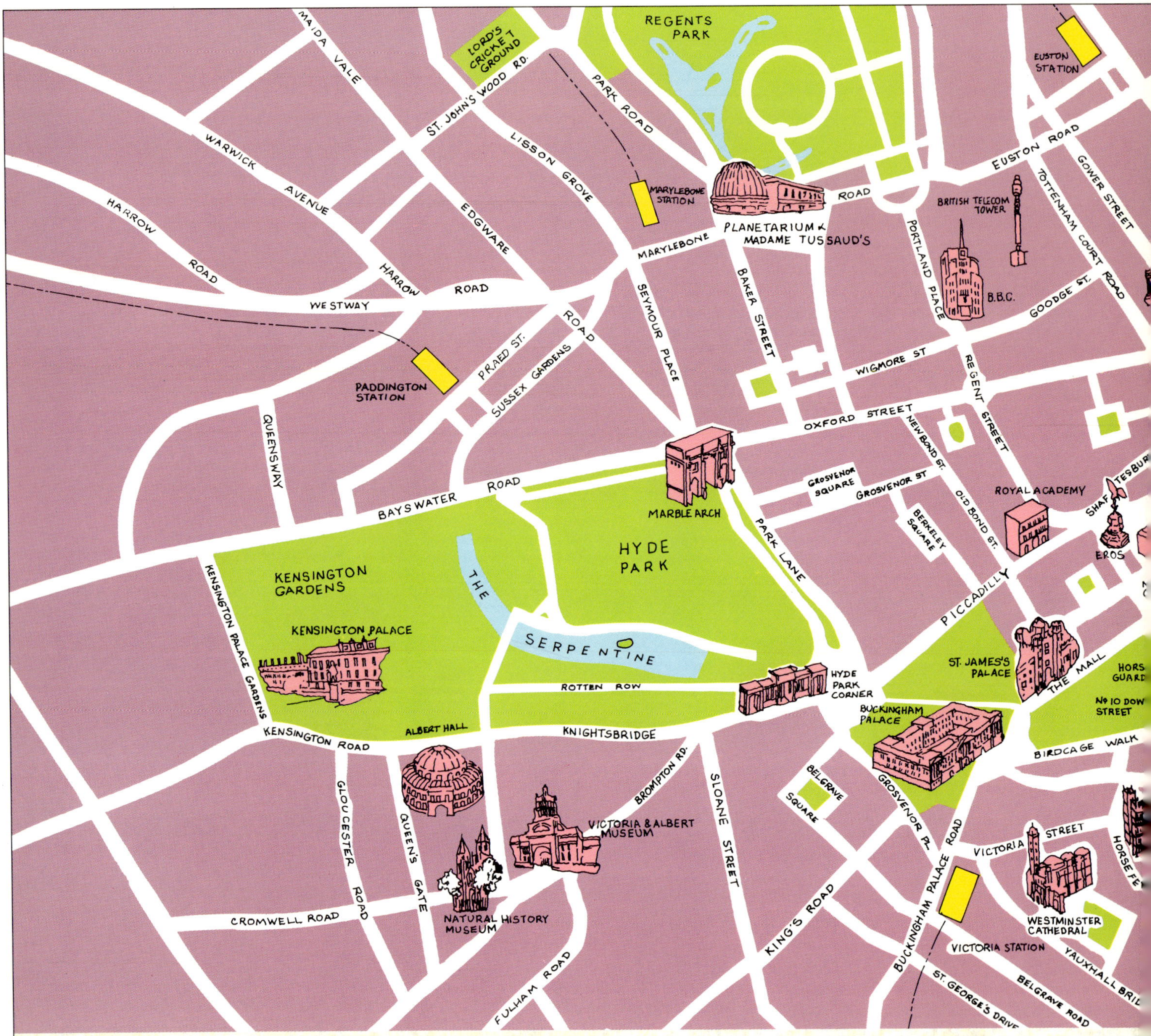

Acknowledgements

Illustrations are reproduced by kind permission of the following: front cover, pp. 8 above right, 10, 11, 12 (both), 22, 23, 25 above right, 26 below, 27 above left and right, Tim Graham Picture Library; Title Page, Peter Sanders; p. 2 left, Photolink; pp. 2 right, 14 above left, 15 above, 19 above, Tony Stone Associates; p. 3 above left and right, back cover, Britain On View Photo Library; p. 3 below left, DOE (Crown Copyright); pp. 4, 6 left, 7, 8 below, 9 right, 18, 21 above, 24 below, 25 below, Brian Shuel; p. 5 left, Colorsport; pp. 5 right, 6 right, 14 above right and below, Split Second; p. 8 left, Bob Langrish; p. 9 left, Photographers International; p. 13 above, Andy Williams; p. 15 below, Pickthall Picture Library; pp. 19 below, 20 below, 24 above, Rex Features; p. 20 above left, Andrew Lawson; pp. 20 right, 25 above left, PictureBank Photo Library; p.21 below, The Photo Source; p. 26 above, Fox Photos; p. 27 below, Robert Harding Picture Library.

Map by Alan Roe.
Designed by Crispin Goodall.
Picture research by Ann Lockhart.

First published by Pitkin Pictorials Ltd, 1989.

Typeset by The Ikthos Studios, Andover, Hampshire.
Printed in Great Britain by ABC Printers, Ditchling, Sussex.

ISBN 0 85372 428 8

For London tourist information, contact THE TOURIST INFORMATION CENTRE, VICTORIA STATION (Tel: 01-730-3488)

189/30

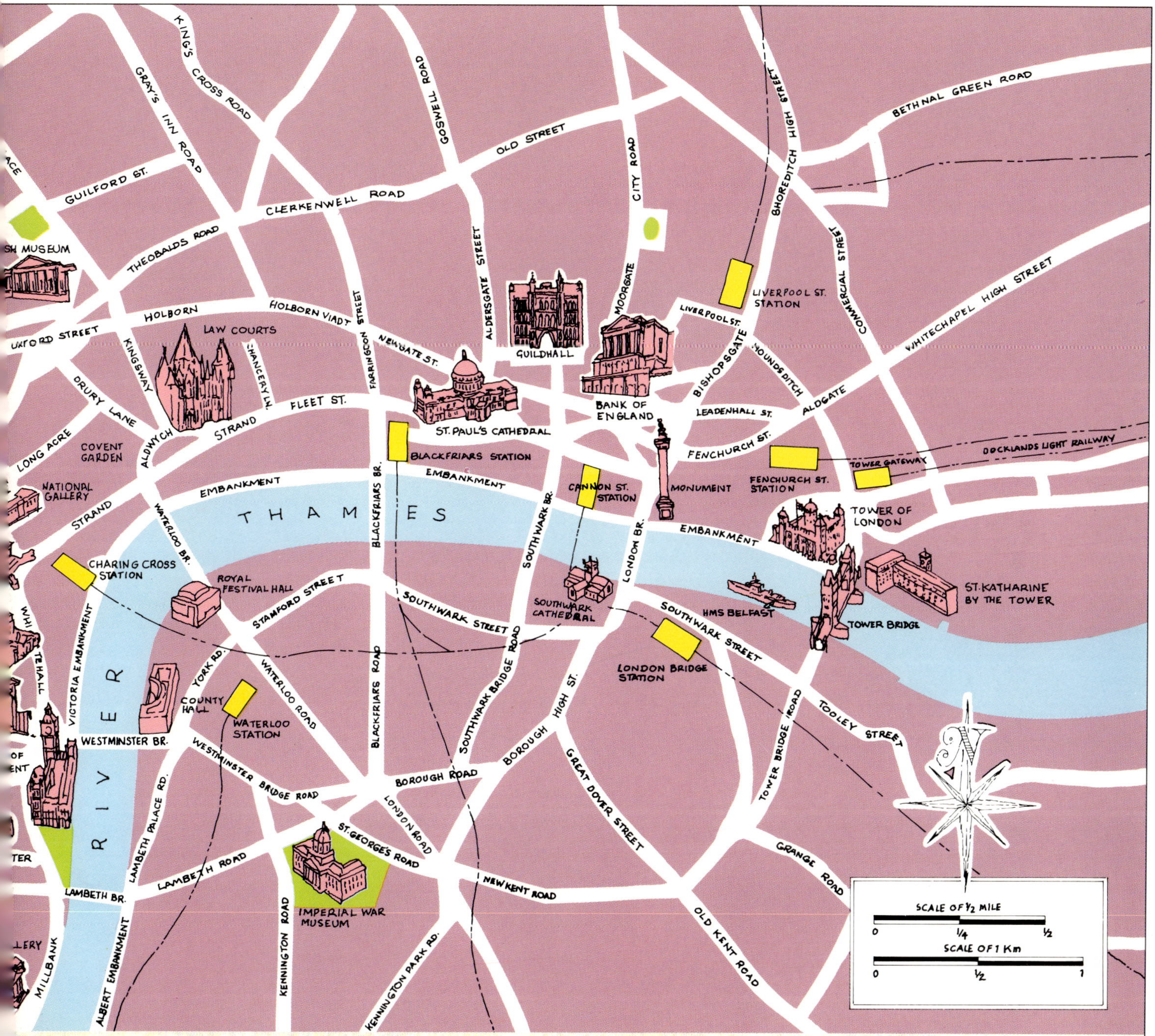
KING'S CROSS ROAD
GRAY'S INN ROAD
GOSWELL ROAD
BETHNAL GREEN ROAD
OLD STREET
CITY ROAD
SHOREDITCH HIGH STREET
GUILFORD ST.
CLERKENWELL ROAD
THEOBALDS ROAD
ALDERSGATE STREET
COMMERCIAL STREET
LIVERPOOL ST. STATION
WHITECHAPEL HIGH STREET
MOORGATE
GUILDHALL
LIVERPOOL ST.
HOLBORN
HOLBORN VIADT
FARRINGDON STREET
NEWGATE ST.
LAW COURTS
KINGSWAY
CHANCERY LN.
BISHOPSGATE
HOUNDSDITCH
DRURY LANE
FLEET ST.
BANK OF ENGLAND
LEADENHALL ST.
ALDGATE
LONG ACRE
COVENT GARDEN
ALDWYCH
STRAND
ST. PAUL'S CATHEDRAL
FENCHURCH ST.
DOCKLANDS LIGHT RAILWAY
BLACKFRIARS STATION
TOWER GATEWAY
NATIONAL GALLERY
EMBANKMENT
BLACKFRIARS BR.
CANNON ST. STATION
MONUMENT
FENCHURCH ST. STATION
THAMES
SOUTHWARK BR.
LONDON BR.
TOWER OF LONDON
WATERLOO BR.
CHARING CROSS STATION
ROYAL FESTIVAL HALL
STAMFORD STREET
SOUTHWARK STREET
SOUTHWARK CATHEDRAL
HMS BELFAST
ST. KATHARINE BY THE TOWER
TOWER BRIDGE
VICTORIA EMBANKMENT
YORK RD.
WATERLOO ROAD
BLACKFRIARS ROAD
SOUTHWARK BRIDGE ROAD
LONDON BRIDGE STATION
BOROUGH HIGH ST.
TOOLEY STREET
RIVER
COUNTY HALL
WATERLOO STATION
WESTMINSTER BR.
WESTMINSTER BRIDGE ROAD
BOROUGH ROAD
GREAT DOVER STREET
TOWER BRIDGE ROAD
LAMBETH PALACE RD.
LONDON ROAD
ST. GEORGE'S ROAD
GRANGE ROAD
LAMBETH ROAD
NEW KENT ROAD
LAMBETH BR.
IMPERIAL WAR MUSEUM
KENNINGTON ROAD
OLD KENT ROAD
KENNINGTON PARK RD.
MILLBANK
ALBERT EMBANKMENT
SCALE OF ½ MILE
0 ¼ ½
SCALE OF 1 Km
0 ½ 1

ISBN 0-85372-428-8
9 780853 724285